STATUE of LIBERTY

(Museum of the City of New York)

STATUE of LIBERTY

CHARLES MERCER

· Updated centennial edition ·

G.P. Putnam's Sons · New York

To
Margaret Frith, Anne Becker, Nora Cohen and Larry Lindner
with respect and affection

2279 - 9589

Copyright © 1985, 1979 by Charles Mercer
All rights reserved. Published simultaneously in Canada by
General Publishing Co. Limited, Toronto.
Printed in the United States of America

Library of Congress Cataloging in Publication Data

Mercer, Charles E.
Statue of Liberty.

Includes index.
SUMMARY: Presents the story behind the building of the
colossal statue in New York Harbor, France's gift to the
U.S. commemorating friendship and symbolizing freedom,
and describes its current renovation.
1. Statue of Liberty National Monument (New York, N.Y.)
—Juvenile literature. 2. Bartholdi, Frédéric Auguste,
1834-1904—Juvenile literature. 3. New York (N.Y.)—
Monuments—Juvenile literature. [1. Statue of Liberty
National Monument (New York, N.Y.) 2. Bartholdi, Frederic
Auguste, 1834-1904. 3. Sculptors] I. Title.
F128.64.L6M44 1985   974.7′1   84-26574
ISBN 0-399-20670-1
ISBN 0-399-21231-0 (pbk.)
Second Impression

Front cover photograph © Peter B. Kaplan, 1984
Back cover photograph courtesy of the Rare Book Division,
New York Public Library

CONTENTS

I
MOST FAMOUS MONUMENT

America's most famous monument, the Statue of Liberty, attracts more than one million visitors a year to its tiny island in New York Harbor. They come from everywhere. Sometimes you hear a half-dozen languages among those who crowd the excursion boats plying between the Statue and New York City's Battery. Midwestern farm families rub elbows with Japanese tourists; a crowd of Maryland high school students laughs with a tour group from Scandinavia; two Israeli youths from Tel Aviv chat with a young couple from Boston.

The mood of the hundreds aboard one of these boats is festive as they pull out from the Battery at the tip of Manhattan. The sky is bright, the tide runs strong, gulls wheel in the boat's wake. Off to starboard, as the boat throbs down the bay, lies an island where deserted brick and concrete buildings sprawl. It is Ellis Island, which for many years was the American reception center for millions of immigrants from Europe.

But the attention of most passengers is on the Statue, which rises ahead on little Liberty Island. Gradually the crowd grows quieter. By the time the boat circles to the island pier nearly everyone is silent. There she stands, America's best known lady, staring gravely across the great harbor.

A little girl speaks: "Why doesn't she look happier?"

No one answers the question because no one knows why.

What is the magic that the Statue of Liberty exercises as strongly today as she has for nearly a century? Of course there is the brief and pleasant boat excursion to an island that offers dramatic views of the New York skyline and the shores of the world's greatest harbor. But it is more than a boat ride that draws more visitors to the Statue of Liberty than any American place of historic significance except the Capitol and the White House in Washington, D.C.

Certainly her size is colossal and her construction unique. The excellent National Park Service guides on Liberty Island offer visitors fascinating statistics about the Statue. The mammoth 151-foot figure raised on a 65-foot base and an 89-foot granite pedestal towers 305 feet above the water. The Statue's mouth is 3 feet wide, each eye 2½ feet across, her forefinger 8 feet long with a fingernail measuring 10 by 13 inches.

But size alone does not account for Liberty's popularity.

Could it be her great age? She was dedicated and opened to the public in 1886. Now her once gleaming copper body and gown have turned green from long exposure to salt air and fierce winds. But there are many older monuments than the Statue in the United States that never have attracted a fraction of as much attention.

Does public interest come from the fact that the Statue symbolizes the liberty that everyone wants as much today as people have wanted throughout history?

All these factors make the Statue of Liberty the popular monument that she is. Anything as popular will, of course, have all sorts of things happen to it. The Statue has been satirized, commercialized, caricatured, scorned, admired, and used by all manner of causes from the raising of money to help fight World War I to the feminist movement of the 1970s to the promoting of a bad Hollywood movie.

Whatever the apparent reasons for so much interest in this huge figure of copper and steel, one fact shines through all: The Statue of Liberty is the symbol of the United States of America to foreigners and Americans alike. Yet her creation was not all romance, glamour and patriotism. Indeed, she came close to never being built at all. Her birth and development took tremendous effort by people from two nations—France and the United States. As is true in achieving the human liberty that the monument symbolizes, the Statue became a reality only after long struggle.

2
YOUNG BARTHOLDI

Americans could not have won their liberty from Britain without French aid. The government of French King Louis XVI began to help the American colonies in the 1770s during the American Revolution, when America was fighting the British government of King George III.

King Louis XVI did not like the idea of American liberty. He was a very dull person who cared about little but hunting and left the work of government to his ministers. They, knowing that France was in a worldwide struggle for power against Britain, saw that they could help the French cause by aiding the American colonies. Their motives were entirely selfish for France—not idealistic for American liberty.

French help in the form of arms, ships, money and men enabled the Americans to form an independent country. One who came to help during the American Revolution was the French Marquis de Lafayette, a young aristocrat who became an American general and a very close friend of George Washington's. The French never forgot how their country helped America win its liberty from Britain. They saw the deep friendship between Lafayette and Washington as symbolic of friendship between the French and American peoples.

Soon after the Americans won their freedom and the United States became an independent nation, France had a revolution too. It was far more bloody and savage than the American Revolution. In the French Revolution the poorest people, most of whom had nothing but the clothes on their backs, revolted against the aristocrats, who had everything. King Louis XVI, his queen, Marie Antoinette, and thousands of aristocrats and their followers were put to death.

After the Revolution there were many changes in government over many years. Leaders came and went. One, Napoleon Bonaparte, conquered most of Europe for France—and then was defeated by the British and Germans. Through wars, violence and changes, many of the French saw the United States as having a perfect government. Why, they wondered, could not France achieve a stable democratic government like that across the Atlantic?

One of those who felt so about America was a young French sculptor, Frédéric Auguste Bartholdi, who earned his first success when nineteen years old. Bartholdi, who never used his first name, had been born into a well-off middle-class family in Colmar, a town in the eastern French province of Alsace, on August 2, 1834. He began studying art when young, and by the time he was eighteen he had his own studio in Paris.

Auguste Bartholdi

Friends often remarked on two aspects of Auguste Bartholdi's personality. As a person he had tremendous enthusiasm for life and work. And as a sculptor he loved *bigness* in art. That was apparent from the heroic size of his first major work, a figure he had been commissioned to do by the town fathers of his native Colmar. It was of General Jean Rapp, said to have been one of Bonaparte's bravest generals. Bartholdi made Rapp 12 feet tall, with feet planted widely and defying his enemies.

Bartholdi's friends told him, "Very effective, Auguste, but how are you going to get this thing out of your studio without knocking down a wall?"

"Stop worrying," Auguste replied. The statue could be moved out the studio's high doors.

However, his friends did not believe so. When Auguste finished the statue he decided to try something before sending it off to Colmar. In those days, if a French artist wanted to be widely acclaimed, he had to have his work shown at and approved by the art establishment, which was called the Salon. So, Auguste thought, before shipping General Rapp off to Colmar, why not take him to the great gallery of the Salon, where critics might praise him?

"Very good, Auguste," agreed his friends. "But wherever you send this statue, how are you going to get it out of this studio?"

"It's easy," said Auguste, summoning workmen and a big dray cart. While a crowd of friends watched, the workmen put wheels under the statue and began to tug at it. Suddenly everyone burst into cheers as the workmen rolled the statue out of the studio with an inch to spare.

Over the cobbled streets of Paris rumbled General Rapp in his horse-drawn dray, accompanied by his creator with friends and helpers. From another direction, in another dray, came the General's pedestal, which was almost 14 feet tall. Outside the Salon the workmen, using pulley hoists, riveted the general to his pedestal. From the watching crowd came exclamations of approval of the statue's heroic height of almost 26 feet after it was mounted on the pedestal.

The workmen hauled the great pedestaled statue to the doors of the gallery. But then the admiration of the watching crows turned into gales of laughter. The statue was too big to get into the Salon. While nearly everyone was laughing, Auguste came close to tears.

Then he thought of something. It seemed that in a crisis he *always* thought of something. He would arrange to have General Rapp left outside, close to the gallery entrance, where all who came and went would see him.

Amusing stories appeared in the newspapers about the statue's being too big to fit into the Salon. Yet all the publicity caused people to come and see General Rapp whether or not they went into the gallery. Influential art critics could not help but see him; some who at first had laughed at the predicament of the artist now praised his work. Thus Auguste Bartholdi won his first success before he was twenty years old.

Not long afterward Bartholdi took a trip to Egypt with young artist friends. The food, the flies, the heat, the diarrhea were awful, but Bartholdi was enchanted. Loving bigness, he never had experienced anything as big as Egypt. The Pyramids, the Sphinx, the Nile, the land—all were fascinating in their great size.

Sometimes Bartholdi bored his friends by marveling at things like: think how it took 100,000 men ten years just to make a pathway to transport the stones for the largest pyramid! But friends always forgave his enthusiasm because he was so passionately fond of life and people. He always would be close to those who liked big ideas, big challenges.

On his trip to Egypt he met a fellow Frenchman, Ferdinand de Lesseps, who wanted to build a canal from the Mediterranean to the Red Sea, thereby saving ships sailing between East and West from going thousands of miles around Africa. Most people scoffed at de Lesseps' plan to pierce the desert sands of the Isthmus of Suez with a canal, but Bartholdi admired the idea.

He decided he would like to create a huge statue to serve as a lighthouse at the entrance to the proposed Suez Canal. Twice the size of the Sphinx, Bartholdi's statue would be the figure of an Egyptian peasant. These peasants, called *fellahin*, did all the hard, dirty work in Egypt, as black slaves did in America. In theory they were free, but they worked like slaves and lived in the worst poverty. Bartholdi wanted his statue to represent not some powerful head of government but the poor, anonymous *fellah*, who for centuries had been toiling in Egypt.

Bartholdi's concern for the plight of the downtrodden everywhere was shared by many French people who did not belong to the aristocracy. Some of these, like Bartholdi, were intellectuals. Others were middle-class trade and small business people who were called the *bourgeoisie*. These people admired America and romanticized it. The one blot they saw on the United States was the slavery of blacks in the South. When the American Civil War broke out, the bourgeois recognized it as a crucial test of whether democratic government was strong enough to hold the nation together and wipe out slavery. They revered Abraham Lincoln and wanted the Union to win and slavery to be destroyed.

Their feelings were not shared by the ruler of France, Emperor Napoleon III, and other European heads of state. These rulers feared the democracy of the United States as a dangerous germ that might infect their own people, who would then drive them out of power. They wanted the Secessionists to win the American Civil War and demonstrate to the world that democracy was too weak a form of government to survive serious strain. Of all the Eu-

[15]

ropean leaders, none was more avid for power than Napoleon III. A nephew of the dead Napoleon Bonaparte, he was a vain, clever adventurer who never stopped plotting against others and had tricked the French into crowning him emperor.

There was great grief in France over President Lincoln's assassination after the Union won the Civil War. A public subscription was started for a solid gold medal to be presented to Lincoln's widow. Napoleon III, fearing such a democratic gesture, displayed the pettiness typical of tyrants. He had his agents destroy the list of subscribers and seize the money, which doubtless found its way into his own pocket. Eventually a medal from Lincoln's French admirers did reach his appreciative widow. But the medal had to be made in Switzerland, sneaked into France to the American ambassador, and then slipped secretly to the United States in a diplomatic pouch. Such was the lack of freedom in the tawdry empire of Napoleon III.

Bartholdi, like all of his close friends, had deep feelings about these events and was closely caught up in them. As did he, the most intelligent people of his time in France wished for a moderate democratic government in their country. One was Édouard-René Lefebvre de Laboulaye, a noted lawyer, teacher and historian of democracy. For years Laboulaye worked quietly to prepare for a democratic government in France modeled somewhat after that of the United States.

One evening in 1865, following the Union victory in the American Civil War, Laboulaye invited a number of friends to his estate near Versailles for dinner. Among them was Bartholdi, whose efforts to create a large monument to the *fellah* at the entrance to the Suez Canal had come to nothing because no one would defray its great cost. (De Lesseps, however, had begun work on the canal itself in 1859; it would take ten years to complete.) Laboulaye, speaking directly to Bartholdi while the other dinner guests listened, said he had had an inspiration. Wouldn't it be wonderful if people in France gave the United States a great monument as a lasting memorial to independence and thereby show that the French government was also dedicated to the idea of human liberty?

With that suggestion Laboulaye set in motion an idea that would result in the Statue of Liberty. To Bartholdi it presented the opportunity to finally build a great statue dedicated to the ideals he believed in. But strange events would occur before Laboulaye's inspiration became the huge monument that stands today in New York Harbor.

3
A MILITARY DISASTER

Like most enthusiastic people, Auguste Bartholdi was persuasive and pursued his goals single-mindedly. He was eager to start plans for a big American monument, but Laboulaye said it was not yet time. Meanwhile, Bartholdi worked hard as a sculptor at other projects.

Bartholdi's zest for life made him popular wherever he went. He was a striking young man, with dark hair, a moustache and little goatee, who was attractive to women. But in his early years he gave no thought to marriage. He was devoted to his widowed mother and did not like to be separated from her for long. When Madame Bartholdi could not come to Paris, Auguste would go home to Colmar, where he maintained a second studio. Much as he enjoyed social life in Paris, he preferred to be at the comfortable Bartholdi home in Colmar with Mama, as he called his mother.

No one loved Charlotte Bartholdi as much as Auguste did; in truth, few even liked her. To nearly everyone but Auguste her manner was cold, her mind condescending. Friends who thought she dominated Auguste unfairly took pains never to tell him so. Madame Bartholdi had grown up a Protestant in a mainly Roman Catholic community, and somehow the experience had turned her into a religious bigot. When Auguste's older brother, Charles, fell in love with a young Jewish woman in Colmar, Madame angrily forbade him to marry her. After that Charles turned bitter, had emotional upsets and never realized his early promise as an artist. As the years passed, he caused increasing problems for his mother and brother with his emotional outbursts. Auguste, ever loyal to both, did not seem to realize that perhaps his mother's decision was the cause of his brother's lifelong emotional disturbance.

When Auguste was born in Colmar, Paris had been several days distant by horse-drawn coach. But by 1860 he could make the trip in a day by train. Though Auguste and his friends did not like the repressive government of the emperor, they had to admit that under his reign France was enjoying healthy economic growth with the aid of railroads. Basically, as was true in the United States during those years, France remained an agricultural country. Farmers tilled every available acre and cared little about what happened in Paris or the world at large. The focus of rural life was the village, with its marketplace and church.

However, with the spread of the railroad, the country was drawn closer to the cities, distances shortened and life in Paris brought nearer. The same was happening in the United States. Yet in America the construction of railroads was generally easier because there was more level land in most of the eastern states than in France, which had much hilly country cut by many deep valleys. In those years the single greatest curb to the increase of railroads was the fact that engines could pull a load up only the slightest incline. Thus roadbeds had to be as level as possible, requiring the construction of tunnels through mountains, and bridges across valleys. Some of the valleys that had to be bridged in France presented tremendous engineering problems involving long distances, great heights, strong winds.

When Auguste Bartholdi traveled rather quickly by train between Paris and Colmar he was aware that the level tracks crossed some deep valleys. In Paris he had met the man who was the greatest builder of railroad bridges in France: Alexandre Gustave Eiffel, best remembered today for the great steel-webbed Eiffel Tower rising 984 feet over Paris, which he completed in 1889. Bartholdi was mindful of Eiffel's accomplishments in building railroad bridges: that he had developed continuous girder constructions which were longer than anything ever done before; that one of his bridge specialties was of huge, two-hinged arches erected without center supports; that another of his specialties was building tall, spidery pylons to support his bridges. Mindful though Bartholdi was of Eiffel's work as he traveled by train across the great engineer's bridges, he had no idea at the time that Eiffel one day would have a crucial role in his own life and work.

The growth of French railroads during those years was enormous. In 1842 there were only 360 miles of tracks, but by 1870 there were 11,250 miles. Better transportation encouraged an increase in manufacture. Large credit institutions and joint-stock banks were formed and speculation boomed. As overseas trade almost quadrupled between 1851 and 1869, France began to emerge as a major industrial nation.

Wise political observers like Laboulaye saw, however, that France's increased wealth was concentrated in the hands of a very few. Sometimes the wealth of the very few in contrast to the poverty of the very many seemed as flagrant as in the past century, before the French Revolution destroyed Louis XVI and his government. Laboulaye believed the government of Napoleon III could not continue for long. But neither he nor anyone foresaw how suddenly and violently change would sweep over France.

It began in July 1870, when Napoleon III stumbled into what became known as the Franco-Prussian War. The French thought that a war against the group of states forming the new nation of Germany would be a pushover. After all, France had a noble military tradition and the emperor's friends said he was a military genius. Within a few weeks, however, the French discovered the awful truth about their military condition.

French generals were old and tired. Military equipment was outmoded, and the men in the ranks were not enthusiastic soldiers. Napoleon III himself was so ill with kidney stones that it took three strong men to lift his fat body onto a horse. Nevertheless, he sat on horseback and took command of the French army gathered in the eastern provinces of Alsace and Lorraine. The Germans attacked; the French were badly confused. A French general wired the War Office in Paris: "Arrived at Belfort. Cannot find my brigade. Cannot find my divisional commander. Do not know where my regiments are. What shall I do?" The War Office didn't know what to tell him. Confusion extended all the way to the top. French generals found with dismay that their commander in chief, far from being a military genius, could not even read a military map.

Bartholdi, enthusiastic patriot, enlisted at once in the National Guard, which was composed of civilians who served as part-time soldiers. Apparently he was at his persuasive best. For, though lacking even an hour of military training, he persuaded the army to make him a major. He was given staff duty in Paris, where he had nothing to do. He did not worry about his mother in Colmar because the emperor's headquarters in the eastern provinces reported stunning French victories. But then, suddenly, Napoleon III sent word to prepare for the defense of Paris. The earlier reports of victories had been

Napoleonic sham. Bartholdi, worried about his mother's safety, persuaded his superiors to give him a three-month leave from his nonexistent duties so that he could prepare the defenses of Colmar.

He wanted to rush home, but war had destroyed the railroad schedules. As his train crept east, delayed for long hours on sidings, Auguste began to see signs of war that dismayed him. A train of wounded soldiers rumbled toward Paris from the front. Roads were choked with people carrying what belongings they could as they fled before the German advance. For the first time Auguste recognized war in all its tragedy. Those uniforms and bands and parades in Paris had been only a little light opera trying to disguise the tragic human experience of war. At last, days after departing Paris, he left the train and began walking toward Colmar. Tired though he was, when his town came in view, Auguste broke into a run.

Colmar was strangely, almost ominously quiet. Madame Bartholdi greeted Auguste calmly, as if nothing out of the way was happening. Birds sang in the beautiful garden behind their house. At the foot of the garden the River Lauch flowed along, as always, toward a fold in the Vosges hills. Surely there was no truth to the rumor the Germans were about to attack this serene place.

But that was the rumor, and Auguste's orders were to link up all available members of the National Guard with regular army units to defend Colmar. Mounting a horse, he rode off in search of regular army units. He could not find any. Returning to Colmar, he found that members of the National Guard chose to make themselves unavailable; they had decided to sit out this phase of the war as civilians. Angrily, eloquently, Auguste rallied a few and dug up arms for them. Military drill was mainly a mystery to him, but he tried to drill his men anyway.

Suddenly word came that the Germans had captured Napoleon III and that a French army of 70,000 had surrendered at Sedan in Alsace.

Auguste formed up the few civilian soldiers who would answer his summons and addressed passionately patriotic words to them: Let everybody else surrender, but the men of Colmar never! They would die fighting for their town! *En avant!*

Another message came: Five thousand German troops were advancing on Colmar. Again Auguste formed his men. They numbered less than 100 now. Nevertheless, *en avant!* By the time they had marched to the outskirts of town, they numbered less than a score.

The situation was hopeless. Auguste burst into angry tears. A few hours later he surrendered Colmar to the Germans.

The German conquerors turned out to be not the bestial monsters predicted. A squad of them was billeted in the Bartholdi house. They were mostly good-natured farm boys who were somewhat embarrassed by the role of conquerors. Madame Bartholdi frightened them by the way she cut them dead when they tried to make conversation. But what a nuisance they were, clumping in and out of the house at all hours and washing their underwear in the river and hanging it to dry in Madame's rose garden.

Auguste could not stand it. His beloved town, even his precious home invaded by an enemy! He had lost his freedom as much as if he were in chains! Now he understood what Laboulaye had meant in saying that liberty never comes easily to anyone.

Much as he wanted to stay with his mother, he had to go. His mother urged him to leave since he was so distraught that she feared he would have a breakdown. Paris was surrounded by the German army, so Auguste made his way to Tours, where the politician Léon Gambetta was trying to organize a new French army. After a while he became an aide to the Italian patriot and "freedom fighter," Giuseppe Garibaldi, who had brought a force of Italian volunteers to aid the French now that Napoleon's army had surrendered to the Germans and the emperor had been eliminated as head of government.

The famous, white-bearded Garibaldi fascinated Auguste with his tales of derring-do and his exile in America. In a hard winter of confused fighting when the French finally went down defeated before stronger, better-led German troops, Auguste endured bitterness, cold, hunger, pain. At last he understood the high price of liberty.

Napoleon III went into exile in England, where he died before long. Germany imposed harsh victory terms on France. In Paris, which had endured months of German seige, the poor and the politically vanquished of many persuasions revolted. They finally were put down by moderate French forces in savage street fighting.

When Bartholdi returned to the shambles of Paris in the spring of 1871, his friend Laboulaye called the political situation "a moment when a bewildered France searches for its way but does not find it." In victory Germany took the provinces of Alsace and Lorraine, making their residents German citizens, and exacted a fearsome toll in money from the French people. Industry was in ruins, agriculture and transportation disrupted. A variety of political faiths vied for power while most of the French, wanting peace and stability, were weary and disgusted.

Out of this agony and confusion there began to be born a new and more democratic French government. It didn't just happen. Like all political developments, it represented the hard efforts and compromises of many. It was called the Third Republic (there having been two previous attempts at similar government). Patterned somewhat after the government of the United States, it would endure until 1940 when, in World War II, Germany defeated France again before the Nazis went down to defeat before the United States, Britain and Russia.

In the emotionally charged spring of 1871, however, the Third Republic still was only an idea that would take a few years of struggle to shape into reality. And it was during that cold, wet spring in Paris that the Statue of Liberty first became a real possibility.

As Laboulaye explained it to Bartholdi, a great monument would advance the cause of French moderate republicans who were striving for creation of the Third Republic. If the French gave the Americans such a magnificent monument, it would forge a link with the United States, which had just triumphed over its own internal enemies in the Civil War and soon would celebrate the 100th anniversary of its founding. This monument, given to America, would be a symbol unifying the French people as never before.

The feelings of Laboulaye, Bartholdi and many others about the project were completely sincere. At the same time, however, their idea represented propaganda to win the support of both French and Americans to their own political goal: the founding of the Third Republic. Bartholdi, as he recalled the conversation several years later, replied with great enthusiasm when Laboulaye suggested he visit America:

" 'Go to see that country,' said he (Laboulaye) to me. 'You will study it, you will bring back to us your impressions. Propose to our friends over there to make with us a monument, a common work, in remembrance of the ancient friendship of France and the United States. We will take up a subscription in France. If you find a happy idea, a plan that will excite public enthusiasm, we are convinced that it will be successful on both continents, and we will do a work that will have a far-reaching moral effect.' "

Before Bartholdi left in May 1871, he wrote Laboulaye, "I will try to glorify the Republic and Liberty over there, in the hope that someday I will find it again here."

4
TRIP TO AMERICA

stop —

The French steamship *Pereire* sailed from Le Havre for New York on June 8, 1871, with Auguste Bartholdi, by his own account, the most excited passenger aboard. He was no longer the brash youth who had created General Rapp in bronze, but his capacity for enthusiasm was as great as ever. Though his English was imperfect, his person was so winsome that he made a fine salesman for anything he espoused. His feelings about liberty were no longer theoretical but the result of passionate experience. He knew the bitterness of trying to fight for his notion of freedom . . . and losing. He knew the anxiety of exile: his adored home literally possessed by an enemy that in effect held his beloved mother captive.

Bartholdi's account of his stormy thirteen-day passage to New York is that of an artist struggling to sketch the perfect monument—and failing day after day. The voyage of the *Pereire*, as reported by Bartholdi, was marked by a wake of the sketches he cast overboard. At last, said Bartholdi, on the final morning when the ship entered New York Harbor, "I saw the New World in a pearly radiance." In the upper harbor he saw tiny Bedloe's Island with its old gray-walled fort. Suddenly, he said, he was inspired by the idea that there— voilà!—was the perfect site for his monument. The inspired artist thereupon sketched in minutes the image that had eluded him for thirteen days. What he sketched was the figure of a huge robed woman holding aloft a torch that represented liberty.

Perhaps it really happened that way. Certainly it was a dramatic way for an artist later to describe his inspiration of the moment when the hat was being passed to pay for his work. However, Marvin Trachtenberg, a noted critic of art and architecture, has pointed out that years previously Bartholdi was sketching similar figures of a woman *fellah* for his ill-fated gigantic statue at the entrance to the Suez Canal. Trachtenberg also explains that the idea of a robed Goddess of Liberty is at least as old as the third century B.C., when the Roman republic built a temple to her. Since that time the figure of a robed woman had often been employed to symbolize prized religious or political virtues.*

So Bartholdi was not bearing a brand-new idea when he went ashore in New York with a rough sketch of a future Statue of Liberty, which he called "Liberty Enlightening the World."

Life for the majority of people in the America Bartholdi visited was far from being the wonderful experience the artist and his Parisian friends imagined. It could be argued, indeed, that most Americans were no better off than were most of the French. It was true the United States did not have a king or dictator, but tyranny can wear guises other than a crown. If you accept one of the dictionary's definitions of liberty as "the power to do as one pleases,"

*Marvin Trachtenberg, *The Statue of Liberty*, New York, The Viking Press, 1976.

A bronze by Bartholdi of his first model for the head of the Statue of
Liberty.

(*left*) An early terracotta statuette of the statue done by Bartholdi.
(*Museum of the City of New York*)

(*right*) This statue model rendered by Bartholdi in 1879 was known as the "American Committee Model."
(*Museum of the City of New York*)

then only a very few and very rich Americans enjoyed that privilege.

While all American blacks recently had been declared free, almost all were the slaves of desperate poverty, little or no employment, practically no education. Women did not even have the right to vote, and most were drudges in the households of their husbands. As in France, the majority of Americans in 1871 led provincial lives on farms or in small villages, where neighbors helped one another, the church was the most influential institution, and the only public building and service was a one-room schoolhouse.

But in America more than in France cities were growing, industry thriving, a middle class increasing in strength. For example, in 1860 there were only sixteen American cities with populations of more than 50,000, but by 1900 there were seventy-eight—and New York had grown larger than Paris. Some of the newcomers to the cities were from American farms and villages, but more were immigrants from overseas. In 1871, when Bartholdi paid his first visit, about 200,000 migrants arrived from Europe. Their numbers would grow until they averaged close to 400,000 a year in the 1880s and 1890s. In the earlier years they came mainly from the British Isles, especially Ireland, and from Germany and northern Europe. Later the balance of migration swung to Italians and southern Europeans. It is interesting that there were far fewer migrants from France than from other European nations.

These immigrants were the *fellahin* of the New World. They built the railroads, dug the coal, did the dirty work for wages sometimes of less than a dollar a day that made a few people—such as the Vanderbilts, Rockefellers, Goulds—very rich and caused the United States to become the leading industrial nation on earth. The migrants lived in abject poverty in awful slums, where they were the prey of all sorts of vultures from pickpockets to politicians. Many died in misery, and some turned to crime in order to survive. But most

[30]

of these *fellahin* of American society had something that the Egyptian *fellah* did not: the hope of bettering one's lot. Everyone in the lower classes knew of some who had made it into the middle classes. And those in the middle classes heard of a few who had made it into the upper classes.

So maybe *liberty* in America was something that scarcely existed in Europe: the *hope* of a better life in which one could do pretty much as he pleased.

Never did the country have a more enthusiastic foreign traveler than Auguste Bartholdi. He spoke so rapturously of it that Americans were flattered and liked him. Laboulaye had seen to it that this effective propagandist for the idea of the Third Republic and a great monument as a gift from France was well spoken for and made good connections on his visit. One "good connection" was John La Farge, a popular and well-to-do artist Bartholdi had met years previously in Paris. Another was Senator Charles Sumner of Massachusetts, powerful chairman of the Senate Foreign Relations Committee, who had won fame as an arch foe of slavery. Sumner, a friend of Laboulaye's who was well versed in French politics and favored the idea of the Third Republic, invited Bartholdi to Washington and introduced him to others of influence there.

Everywhere Bartholdi went he met influential people. In Philadelphia it was an important newspaper publisher. In Boston, the famous poet Henry Wadsworth Longfellow. At La Farge's Newport home he charmed the noted American architect Richard Morris Hunt.

On his own initiative Bartholdi undertook a pilgrimage to the summer White House, which was at Long Branch, New Jersey, that year. There President Ulysses S. Grant prowled the long enclosed porch of a plain clapboard house, puffing on a cigar and staring out to sea. If the little general was a mite surprised when Bartholdi bounded to him, bowing, with talk of a statue celebrating liberty in New York Harbor, he did not show it but treated his French visitor with the courtesy he displayed to nearly everyone. One of the few pleasures Grant had in his summer idleness at Long Branch was when passing ships fired cannon blank charges in salute to him. Thus, when a passing vessel fired its cannon while Bartholdi was talking and the artist leaped in dismay, Grant was delighted. Bartholdi left with the impression the president liked his idea. But there is no record of President Grant commenting on it to associates at the time. Possibly he wondered if Bartholdi was an entertainment thought up by one of his friends to help while away his boredom at Long Branch.

Bartholdi went West. He visited Chicago and Omaha. If a prize had been offered for most untiring foreign tourist of the year, surely he would have won it. He admired the vastness of the prairies he crossed, the hugeness of a wild buffalo herd that held up his train for hours. The soaring Rockies left him almost speechless. And the great size of American families! After a conversation with the Mormon leader Brigham Young in Utah, he wrote his mother a somewhat dazed letter about Young, asking her to try to imagine a man who had sixteen wives and forty-nine children. He went on to San Francisco and thought the Pacific somehow looked bigger than the Atlantic. At last he was taken to see a forest of giant redwoods—and was struck dumb with awe as he never had been in Egypt.

On his way home he wrote another letter to Laboulaye, saying, "Everything in America is big." And at last he broke his long silence on the quality of American food: "Here, even the peas are big."

5

AN AGE OF
MONUMENTS

Like every astute politician, Laboulaye had a fine sense of timing. He had known, of course, that the idea of a statue to "Liberty Enlightening the World" was impossible under Napoleon III; that despot would have jailed anyone who had made such a suggestion. And in the uncertain days after the Franco-Prussian War Laboulaye realized that it would be premature to publicize the idea of a statue. "We must wait until the new Republic becomes a reality," he told Bartholdi when the sculptor returned from the United States and reported the Americans amenable to raising a monument to liberty.

Laboulaye knew that it was as dangerous to hasten the creation of a new French government as to rush the cooking of a French soufflé. Haste could make the whole concoction fall flat. As in the founding of Federal Constitutional government in the United States following the American Revolution, there were many separate French interests to be considered, many political compromises to be worked out. The process had taken a long time in the United States and would take even longer in France. Laboulaye believed that previous French governments had failed in some instances because they had been created too hastily. He felt that if the public had ample time to contemplate the idea of a Third Republic, it might not suffer revulsion upon trying to digest it.

Meantime Bartholdi worked at other projects. One was commissioned by the town of Belfort in Alsace as a monument to its heroic defenders in the Franco-Prussian War. It still can be seen today: the figure of a huge stone lion, expressing rage and defiance, wounded but still dangerous. The figure, about seventy feet long and thirty-five feet high, is set into the cliffs below the town's fortress.

Monuments, like Bartholdi's *Lion of Belfort* and the one he planned to raise to liberty in the United States, were an especially popular form of art in the nineteenth century. Their popularity reflected the fact that it was an age of ostentation, when people delighted in the showy. Monuments sprang up in both Europe and the United States. Visitors flocked to them, like pilgrims to shrines. Someone said statues were being raised at such a rate in Washington that soon there would be no room for live people. Nearly every American village, North and South, had its monument, however modest, to those who had died in the Civil War. It was an age when many a millionaire wanted a family burial monument worthy of a head of state, a time when nearly every politician wanted the memory of himself preserved in bronze or stone.

Nearly all nineteenth century monuments had elements of the classical about them, either in the dress of their subjects or in columns and other architectural details. "Classical" refers to the civilizations of ancient Greece and Rome. Many artists of Bartholdi's time felt that by using classical elements in their work they gave their subjects added strength, endowing them with qualities of the ancients, which had endured the passage of time. The work of those artists was called neoclassical because it was a revival of the classical style.

As Bartholdi worked at small clay models for his proposed liberty statue, he inevitably took a neoclassical view of his design. It was the popular style of his time. His French political backers did not want him to try anything new or daring—and, anyway, it was not in his nature to try new styles. He simply followed the age-old idea of liberty personified as the figure of a woman. Then he dressed her in the robe and sandals of a proper Roman matron of classical times. She is reserved, virtuous, maternal—a mother figure with whom none would quarrel. So as not to make her seem too passive, Bartholdi put a broken chain at Liberty's feet and thrust her left foot forward in a stride intended to show progress from her former bondage.

Another reason for Liberty's left foot being forward was to balance the heavy beacon she holds in her raised right hand. Standing flat-footed, she would have looked awkward. Bartholdi was very careful about that beacon in her hand. If it had been a flaming torch—a traditional revolutionary symbol— the people of moderate politics to whom the statue was meant to appeal (and who were the ones expected to pay for it) might have suspected that Liberty was represented as a firebrand. So Bartholdi changed the historic freedom torch into a beacon welcoming voyagers to America.

In working on the models for his statue he put in Liberty's curved left arm tablets such as female figures carried in past works of religious art. But Bartholdi took pains to steer clear of obvious religious symbols. So the tablets in Liberty's left arm, which offer another balancing effect to the beacon in her right hand, are inscribed in a mixture of English and Latin:

JULY

IV

MDCCLXXVI

July 4, 1776, is, of course, the official date of the signing of the Declaration of Independence.

Around the brow of his statue Bartholdi designed a radiant antique crown of seven spikes. This type of crown was used in Christian religious art of the eighteenth century and symbolized the sun's radiance to the seven planets. But Bartholdi changed that meaning and said that the seven spikes of Liberty's crown were meant to "enlighten" the seven seas and continents of the world.

While Bartholdi was working on models of "Liberty Enlightening the World" between other projects, he fell in love with a beautiful young woman. Her name was Jeanne-Emilie Baheux de Puysieux, and she had been a dressmaker's assistant in the city of Nancy. Auguste said that one of the things that attracted him most to Jeanne-Emilie was her lovely arms. She came to Paris, where she served as his model. The arms of the Statue of Liberty were fashioned after those of Jeanne-Emilie.

She and Auguste loved each other. He kept saying he wanted to marry her, but remembering the fate of his brother Charles and the beloved Jewish girl, he feared to tell his mother. And, said Auguste, he simply could not get married without first telling Mama. Patiently and sympathetically, Jeanne-Emilie kept saying she understood.

Auguste did not want the face of the proposed statue to be as beautiful as Jeanne-Emilie's. He decided he would model the statue's face after that of his mother. Most people thought Madame Bartholdi's expression grim and dour. But Auguste thought his mother's face expressed strength and long-suffering. He intended his statue's face to portray the suffering he thought necessary to achieve human liberty. He meant her to be a martyr. Was he unconsciously memorializing his mother as a great martyr?

Meanwhile, as Bartholdi toiled in his studio, the French inched slowly toward the formation of the Third Republic, with various political interests working out compromises. In 1873 the republicans commissioned Bartholdi to create a statue of Lafayette to be given to the Americans for placing in Union Square in New York. The French idea was that if the Americans were glad to receive Lafayette, they would be even more pleased to accept the much bigger, grander statue of "Liberty Enlightening the World."

When the French politicians talked about "the Americans," they did not refer to the hundreds of thousands of immigrant families living in city slums or those far from the cities in villages and on farms. French leaders were concerned, rather, with that very small portion of the American people who, as a result of money or education or attainment, influenced the attitudes of the United States government. These "opinion makers" of the days before such mass communication media as television, radio and films, were teachers, writers, publishers, legislators, business administrators and the like.

It was the French notion to use their gift of a mammoth Statue of Liberty as propaganda—a kind of intellectual bribe—to those "opinion makers" in the United States who would look kindly on a foreign government that gave the country a big work of art. The influential Americans who welcomed the gift would, in turn, offer the new French government goodwill and moral support and, possibly, through the American government, even more practical benefits. That is, the French who offered the gift stood to gain more than would the Americans who received it. This was a very subtle idea. And it would result in some big surprises.

[37]

6
WORK BEGINS

In 1874 the French Assembly passed a series of laws that together composed the constitution of the Third Republic. Now, Laboulaye told Bartholdi, it was time to begin publicizing the idea of the French giving the Americans a great monument to liberty. Bartholdi could not begin actual work on the statue, of course, because there was no money to pay for it.

By late in the year it was evident that the French could not raise enough money to pay for the huge statue. People in the United States would have to help. While the project had been advertised as a gift from the French, the Americans must help pay for the gift they would receive. It was decided the French would pay for the statue itself, the Americans for its pedestal and foundation. A fund-raising committee called the Franco-American Union was formed, with members from both nations. In France the republican newspapers ran glowing accounts of the project. Bartholdi traveled about making speeches.

[38]

The wealthy were courted, but no sum was deemed too small. Schoolchildren were urged to give their pennies. The children, as usual with interesting projects, gave pennies generously. But no rich Frenchman stepped forward with a large amount of money.

Nevertheless, enough money had dribbled in by November 1875, for the Franco-American Union to give a sumptuous dinner at the Louvre Hotel for wealthy and influential people. The guests listened, spellbound, to Bartholdi describe his projected great work. The amazing thing about the project was not just its enormous size. Just as fabulous to the rapt listeners was the fact you would be able to go *inside* this statue and climb all the way to its top for an eagle's view.

Fortified by Bartholdi's enthusiasm and a good dinner with various wines, the committee told him to go ahead—get started. Some optimistic souls even believed he might finish the project in less than a year so that it could arrive in America in time for the 1876 centennial celebration of the birth of independence.

The place Bartholdi chose for his workshop was the best in Paris: Gaget, Gauthier and Company. Its craftsmen included all sorts of specialists who had made, among other notable things, the statues on the spires of Notre-Dame Cathedral. In order to take on the Liberty job, Gaget, Gauthier expanded its facilities at 25, rue Chazelles.

Bartholdi appeared there early one crisp November morning to describe the monument to the craftsmen who would work on it. He spread his drawings on a huge table where he placed a 4-foot clay model of the statue—the model for which Jeanne-Emilie had been posing. The craftsmen lounged around the table, sipping from mugs of steaming coffee and listening closely while Bartholdi explained the complicated and truly amazing work necessary to create Liberty.

Stone would not do for this statue. It was much too heavy, and cracks in stone joinings would look bad. Neither should bronze be used because it also was very heavy and much too expensive. Since the statue would have to be shipped across the Atlantic, it must be both durable and of relatively light weight. So Bartholdi had decided to use copper. But intricate and difficult things had to be done before the copper experts went to work.

First, the 4-foot clay model on the table would go through three painstaking, progressive enlargements, each involving nearly ten thousand measurements, until it finally achieved the colossal size of the finished statue. Each plaster enlargement included all the various parts of Liberty—her head, her arms, her torso, and so on. Each enlargement would be made in pieces, and all the pieces finally assembled for the completed work.

Carpenters would construct huge wooden frames that carefully followed every contour of the final, full-scale plaster model. Then the copper craftsmen would go to work. Using hammers and levers, they would carefully force into shape extraordinarily thin copper sheeting, which was only 2.5 millimeters— about 1/100th of an inch—thick. Then the shape of the plaster model would be forced into very thin, soft lead sheets. Finally the shape of the copper would be beaten into exactly the shape of the lead sheets.

This method used for creating Liberty was called *repoussé* and was very old. Some of the earliest Greek bronzes which survived into modern times were made of hammered thin sheets of copper riveted together over a wooden core.

As Bartholdi described his plans to the craftsmen in the drafty, high-ceilinged workshop of Gaget, Gauthier, one interrupted to ask how all this intricate copper work would be held together. That brought up one of the most interesting aspects of the construction of the great monument.

All that fine copper work would be only the skin of the Statue of Liberty. What would hold her together and make her withstand the high winds that often swept New York Harbor with gale force would be a skeleton constructed of steel. A system of iron straps would fasten the copper skin to the steel skeleton.

The one volunteering to construct this intricate skeleton was the famous engineer Eiffel, who was renowned for his steel railroad bridges. He took the job not just as a patriotic gesture, but because it challenged his engineering genius. Like Bartholdi, he was fond of the grandiose. Nothing as structurally involved as the Statue of Liberty ever had been imagined before. This elaborate work of very thin copper, in order to withstand pressure and weather, would depend entirely on the strength and balance of its steel frame. Problems involved in the skeleton of the raised arm alone were too much for even skilled structural engineers. But Eiffel delighted in problems that defied others.

A few weeks after work began on the statue it was evident to Bartholdi and Eiffel that it could not possibly be completed in time for the 1876 American centennial celebration of independence. But Bartholdi resolved at least to have the raised arm and beacon completed for showing at the International Centennial Exhibition in Philadelphia. Twenty men toiled ten hours a day, seven days a week to complete the twenty-one pieces composing the arm and hand. Hard though they worked, the section was not finished for the opening of the Exhibition, but it did arrive there before the big fair closed in the fall.

Meanwhile Bartholdi, who was named an official French representative to the Exhibition, left for the United States in May 1876. Besides his work on Liberty, he had long since completed the statue of Lafayette the government had commissioned as a gift to New York and also had designed a fountain which was shown at the Exhibition.

When he arrived in New York he found with dismay that his statue of Lafayette, which had arrived months ahead of him, had not even been uncrated. It needed a pedestal before being placed in Union Square, but no American showed the slightest interest in providing one for the monument to

This is the high-ceilinged workshop of Gaget, Gauthier in Paris where
the Statue of Liberty was constructed.

(Rare Book Division, New York Public Library)

These carpenters are building the huge wooden frames which carefully
followed every contour of the final model.

Here the copper craftsmen carefully force thin sheets into shape on
the wooden frames.

The intricacy of the work shows in this photo of the left hand. Note the workman in the upper right, literally white with dust.

There were three painstaking enlargements of each part of the statue from a starting 4-foot clay model, each involving ten thousand measurements. The final enlargements of the left arm are shown in this extraordinary photograph.

(Rare Book Division, New York Public Library)

Artists were constantly visiting the workshop to make drawings of the progress with Liberty. This was drawn for the French illustrated newspaper *Journal Universel*.

(*Museum of the City of New York*)

A contemporary drawing of work being rushed on the right hand so that it could be shown separately at the 1876 International Exhibition in Philadelphia.

(Museum of the City of New York)

When the head of the statue was finished, it was brought out into the courtyard of Gaget, Gauthier.

Alexandre Gustave Eiffel, con-
structor of the famed Eiffel
Tower in Paris, designed the
steel skeleton on which Liberty
was mounted. Here his work
rises in the courtyard of Gaget,
Gauthier while craftsmen toiled
in the workshop.

(Rare Book Division, New York
Public Library)

The statue begins to take shape on the skeleton from the feet upward.
(*Rare Book Division, New York Public Library*)

For a time the head of Liberty is displayed separately in Paris.

Then the head is brought back to the courtyard as the Statue rises toward completion.

(Rare Book Division, New York Public Library)

This contemporary painting by Victor Dargaud shows the completed
Statue of Liberty and its scaffolding rising above the Paris rooftops.
(*Museum of the City of New York*)

the French hero of the American Revolution. This American indifference to a European work of art might have served as a warning to Bartholdi about the reception of his Statue of Liberty in the United States. But it did not. Instead of blaming the Americans, Bartholdi blamed himself for not having created enough public enthusiasm for his Lafayette. As usual, he scurried around, trying to raise money for the pedestal. But almost a year passed before funds were obtained. Several months after that, Bartholdi's Lafayette was raised in New York's Union Square, where it stands today.

On July 4, 1876, Bartholdi made a trip to Bedloe's Island, the site he had chosen for the big statue on his previous trip to America. Like many artists, he was a bit superstitious. He chose the Fourth of July to visit the island because he hoped that patriotic day might bring luck to his project. He even was pleased to note that the tug which took him down New York Harbor was called *Washington.* A member of the Franco-American Union had managed to dig up a couple of government surveyors to go with him. These surveyors were furious at having to work on a steaming hot national holiday when all citizens were supposed to rest and have fun. Apparently Bartholdi, enthusiastically clambering around old Fort Wood on Bedloe's Island, didn't realize how pained his surveyors felt.

The little island took its name from one Isaac Bedloo, a wealthy Dutch merchant who had owned it in the seventeenth century. Its name was changed from Bedloo to Bedlow and then to Bedloe's before the federal government obtained the place in 1800. The army built star-shaped Fort Wood there, but the cannon mounted on its angular bastions never were fired at an enemy. During the Civil War it served as an ammunition depot and recruiting station, and at various other times it was used as a hospital and quarantine station. By the time Bartholdi visited there, the island served no purpose, the fort had fallen into disrepair and all the guns were gone.

After Bartholdi went ashore he remarked that it would be nice if it were called Liberty Island. This merely brought snarls from the sweating surveyors dragging their equipment around in the glaring sunlight. But usually, for the rest of his life, Bartholdi referred to the site of his statue as Liberty Island. Seventy years later, in 1956, the name of Bedloe's Island finally was changed officially to Liberty Island.

Bartholdi viewed the island with a discoverer's eye as he made swift calculations on the best way to position his Statue of Liberty there. In Paris he had thought that Liberty should be facing down New York Harbor to greet arriving travelers, with her back to the city. But now he realized that would not be right. People who saw her aboard approaching ships would get only a quick head-on view. The ideal way to view Liberty would be when you passed her—as soldiers do a general in review. The realization came to Bartholdi as he stood on a parapet of old Fort Wood while a ship from Europe, decks packed with immigrants, came slowly up the harbor. The immigrants, appearing a solid mass of black in their peasant clothing, stared silently at Fort Wood as their ship passed. In the sun's glare Bartholdi watched the whiteness of hundreds of faces against dark clothing as the people turned to watch the island.

This, he thought, was the way Liberty must face, looking across the main channel that led up the harbor to New York City. Furthermore, if Liberty was pointed in this direction, she would fit better into the outline of the old star-shaped fort, because its channel-side bastion was much wider than the other sides. It did not matter that because of the way the harbor was shaped the statue actually would be facing south by southeast. What mattered was that to those coming to America, Liberty would *appear* to be facing due east to the Old World.

Never had Bartholdi felt so happy. He could *feel* Liberty rising behind him, her beacon held high as she gazed at the passing ship of immigrants. The intense July heat and the grumbling of the surveyors did not matter. As Bartholdi imagined it, his greatest work of art already was completed.

As the tug *Washington* took him and the others back to Manhattan, they passed close to another, larger island a bit north and west of Bedloe's. The trees and fields of its twenty-seven acres were verdantly green. It was called Ellis Island, Bartholdi learned, and had been farmland for generations. The tug churned on up the harbor to the big park at the southern end of Manhattan Island, which was called the Battery. Bartholdi and the others went ashore there close to the large cylindrical-shaped building called Castle Garden.

That was the place the hundreds of thousands of immigrants from Europe passed through. Castle Garden was, someone said, the gateway to a new life in a new world. At that time the federal government did not concern itself with immigration. People from Europe who landed in New York on their way to live in America identified themselves to officers of New York State at Castle Garden. Immigration procedures were the responsibility of the state where a person entered the country. There was no careful "processing" or "screening" of immigrants into the United States until the federal government took over responsibilities for immigration in 1892.

On the Fourth of July when Bartholdi returned from Bedloe's Island, firecrackers popped and banged in Manhattan's Battery Park. But there was no holiday for the officers counting immigrants through Castle Garden. Day after day, seven days a week and fifty-two weeks a year, people poured from Europe into the United States. They seemed never to stop coming. How long, Bartholdi wondered, before there would be a Statue of Liberty to welcome immigrants to America?

[56]

7

MONEY! MONEY!

As Auguste traveled about the northeastern United States trying to help raise money for the statue's pedestal and foundation, he grew lonely for Jeanne-Emilie. One evening he was talking about her to his artist friend John La Farge and John's vivacious wife, Margaret.

Suddenly Margaret asked, Why not send for Jeanne-Emilie and marry her here in America?

Auguste wondered aloud what Mama would say about that.

"How," asked Margaret, "can your mother complain if you're already married?"

But of course! What a simple solution to the problem that had bothered Auguste for such a long time! That very evening he wrote a long letter to Jeanne-Emilie, urging her to take the first available passage to America and marry him.

There are different versions of Auguste's romance with Jeanne-Emilie. But it seems possible that she originally was a Roman Catholic. That would not have troubled Auguste personally much. He himself was more a non-Catholic than a strong Protestant. It was his mother's attitude that caused his problem. Madame Bartholdi might have brought herself to accept a dressmaker's assistant as a daughter-in-law, but a Roman Catholic—never!

If Jeanne-Emilie actually was a Roman Catholic, as has been suggested, she could not have been a devout one. For, upon receiving Auguste's letter proffering marriage, she flew to him in the New World as fast as she could in that age before airplanes. She and Auguste were married in a Protestant service at the La Farges' Newport home.

Auguste still had some quaverings about his mother. In Newport he found a clergyman who was willing to sign a statement to the effect that Jeanne-Emilie was a Unitarian—a Protestant sect, to be sure, though not of Madame's stern Calvinist kind. Then Margaret La Farge had a charming, generous idea. She decided that Jeanne-Emilie was her second cousin who she had introduced to Auguste—and she would write Madame and tell her so. Margaret's presumption, perhaps egotistical, was that if Jeanne-Emilie were a cousin of the La Farges, it would give her a social status that Madame would find acceptable.

Auguste and Jeanne-Emilie did not return to France until January 1877. Whether they would live happily ever after obviously depended on how Mama felt.

Madame came to Paris at once to welcome her adored son home from America and pass judgment on his bride. She started out by trying to tolerate her. But Jeanne-Emilie's nature was so sweet that Madame grew to like her as much as she ever did anyone.

Auguste, delighted that his wife and Mama got along so well, turned his energies to the Statue of Liberty. She became, in fact, a third woman in his life. "My daughter Liberty" he began to call her. Nearly all the craftsmen who worked at Liberty began to have affection for her. Some called her "the old girl." Instead of being a mere thing, the statue became like a real person to those creating her.

Bartholdi wanted Liberty's head completed for display at the Paris World's Fair of 1878. Sometimes, when money was available for wages, as many as fifty men at a time worked on the head. And some days as many visitors stood around the huge workshop gawking at the craftsmen clambering about Liberty's great head like ants on a hill.

One visitor in the fall of 1877 was Ulysses S. Grant, who was on a world tour. The former president, staring up at Liberty's head, reputedly said something about remembering Bartholdi's visit to him at Long Branch. Whatever he actually said, the general couldn't get over the fact that Liberty's eyes were two and one-half feet wide.

The never-ending problem was money. Work often had to be suspended because there was not enough to pay the craftsmen or to buy more materials. The Fair was scheduled to open May 1, 1878, and Bartholdi and the craftsmen pressed hard to have the head completed by that date. But Liberty was destined to be a tardy lady. Her gleaming copper head was not finished till June 1. That day the huge head was placed on the largest dray ever seen in Paris and twelve big horses dragged it to the Fair. Thousands lined the streets to watch.

Though Liberty was a sensation at the Fair, contributions to her creation lagged. While her upraised arm remained in Philadelphia, progress on the rest of her continued very slowly through 1879. Then in 1880 the Franco-American Union had an inspiration. They would hold a lottery. This finally brought in enough money to assure completion of the Statue of Liberty—or so it seemed at first.

Bartholdi was no financial wizard. He kept underestimating costs, perhaps partly from the fear that if he named too high a figure everyone would give up on the project. It's difficult to say how much the completed statue and its pedestal actually cost. People knew what *parts* of the project cost, but the total became as big a jumble as the workshop where Liberty was being created. One problem was that the prices of her basic materials—copper, iron and steel—kept changing. Considering that the statue absorbed 100 tons of copper and 125 tons of steel over many years, with books being kept by many different people, it is hard today to make a firm estimate. In any event, Liberty's record never was besmirched—as have some other public projects—with hints of graft and profiteering.

After the French lottery of 1880, work went faster. Gustave Eiffel started work on the steel skeleton in the courtyard of Gaget, Gauthier, while Bartholdi and the copper craftsmen pounded and shaped the skin inside the workshop. In the summer of 1881 Bartholdi decided it was time to begin putting some skin on Liberty's bones. A ceremony was set for October 24, and on that day the dignified American ambassador to France, Levi Morton, took a sledgehammer from Laboulaye and solemnly drove a rivet into the big toe of Liberty's left foot.

Once begun, the process of clothing Eiffel's skeleton in copper skin from the ground up, went on slowly. By midsummer of 1882 Liberty was dressed in copper to the waist. Bartholdi held a luncheon for several members of the press. Gaily he led them inside the statue and bounded up a series of ladders, with the newspapermen clambering behind him, till they came to a platform where a large table was set. Waiters hauled up food and wine in baskets, and everyone made merry over the fact they were eating lunch on Liberty's knee.

By December of that year Bartholdi was able to write William M. Evarts, the New York lawyer and politician who was in charge of American fund-raising efforts: "The statue commences to reach above the houses, and next spring one will see it overlook the entire city."

Liberty continued to grow, with occasional pauses while more money was raised, until she towered high above the courtyard on the rue Chazelles. Money shortages appear to have been not the only reason for the slow creation of the statue—a pace so slow that it took two and one-half years alone to dress Liberty. The other factor was that the intricate workmanship took much more time than Bartholdi had anticipated. Whatever the difficulties, he seems never to have lost his faith that the statue would be completed. Usually he sprang about the workshop ebulliently. But he had a rare week of sadness in the winter of 1883/1884 when Laboulaye died before his treasured project was finished.

At last Liberty received her final touches in June 1884, and Bartholdi and the Franco-American Union prepared to give her officially to the United States. It was a fine ceremony, with speeches and music . . . all the pomp and circumstance that people enjoyed in those days. Ambassador Morton accepted Liberty with the great solemnity that marked everything he did. After receiving the statue, he came close behind as Bartholdi led the way for an official inspection tour of the statue's interior. Around a central steel column wound two sets of stairways, one for climbing up and the other for going down. Morton said later that it was dark inside "with nothing to guide our steps but the thousand and one little eyelets of sunlight that came through the rivet holes."

Bartholdi sprang ahead, agile as a monkey, his excitement over the occasion making him seem to float upward in the darkness. Someone far behind in the party called up to him, asking him how many steps there were to the top of this thing. He called back that there were only 168. Groans greeted his remark. Many people began to cross over to the descending stairway. Ambas-sador Morton, huffing and puffing, made it all the way. But not many others did. Bartholdi was very disappointed to see how few climbed to the top with him.

He assumed that work was progressing on the Bedloe Island site where Liberty would stand. Sometimes weeks passed without his receiving any clear report on the situation from his American friends. But he believed they were as enthusiastic as he about the project and he had faith they would overcome their difficulties with base and pedestal as he had overcome many difficulties in creating the statue.

While a home was being prepared for her, Liberty remained in Paris through autumn and winter. She was hostess to a constant stream of visitors who climbed up and down her stairways and admired her huge size. One visitor on a winter day was the great novelist Victor Hugo, now aged, ailing, still the most revered Frenchman of his time. He and Bartholdi talked for a while about their old mutual friend, Laboulaye, and how sad it was that he had died before the statue was completed. Then Victor Hugo, frail though he was, said he wanted to climb to the top of the Statue of Liberty. It took a whole crowd of his friends to stop him.

On May 13, 1885, Victor Hugo wrote an inscription for a booklet about the statue:

"To the sculptor form is everything and is nothing. It is nothing without the spirit—with the idea it is everything."

Possibly they were the last words Hugo ever wrote, for he died eight days later. Bartholdi treasured the lines to the end of his life.

Spring came to Paris early in 1885. Liberty stopped receiving visitors. It was time she was sent to America. The craftsmen who had laboriously con-structed her began the equally hard task of dismantling her into pieces for the long ocean voyage.

[62]

The efforts to raise funds for construction of the Statue of Liberty and its pedestal and base continued for years in the United States and France. Part of the fund-raising campaign was this display of the right hand at the 1876 International Exhibition in Philadelphia.

(Museum of the City of New York)

An 1885 engraving by W. S. Taylor depicts constructing the base of the statue. The view to the north shows Manhattan and Brooklyn, joined by the Brooklyn Bridge.

(*Museum of the City of New York*)

An artist's concept of the joyous celebration in New York Harbor when the French transport *Isere* arrived on June 17, 1885, with the dismantled parts of the Statue of Liberty. This was the cover illustration on the French periodical *L'Illustration* on July 11, 1885.

(*Museum of the City of New York*)

Constructed in Paris, then taken apart to be shipped across the Atlantic, the Statue of Liberty had to be reassembled again on its island site. This 1886 illustration from *Frank Leslie's Magazine* shows workmen putting finishing touches on the inside of the statue.

(*Museum of the City of New York*)

An unknown artist's concept of the reconstructing of the statue as seen from the exterior. This engraving appeared in the French illustrated newspaper *Journal Universel*.

(Museum of the City of New York)

Edward Moran's oil painting is his impression of the scene of celebration after the statue finally was unveiled.

Suddenly many people didn't want to see Liberty leave France. She had been conceived and born and grown up in Paris, and it seemed only right she should live out her natural life there. But a promise had been made to the Americans—and the promise had to be kept.

A group of Americans living in Paris understood how the French dreaded to see Liberty go, so they made a thoughtful gesture. They had a thirty-five-foot model of Bartholdi's Statue of Liberty cast in bronze as a memorial to the French people for what they had done in sending their great monument to the United States. The smaller replica of Liberty stands today in Paris on a tiny island of the Seine river. The Isle of Swans, as the island is called, is just downstream from the Eiffel Tower.

The work of dismantling and crating Liberty went on carefully under Bartholdi's supervision. It was like taking apart a giant jigsaw puzzle that would have to be reassembled on the other side of the Atlantic. Each piece was marked with a special number or figure and all joining edges of the pieces were designated by the same sign. Altogether, 214 huge crates of many shapes were required to ship the parts of the statue.

A special train of seventy cars carried the crates to the river port of Rouen. There they were carefully loaded aboard the *Isere*, a sturdy transport of the French navy that had been assigned the task of transporting the dismantled statue to New York. *Isere* sailed from Rouen on May 22, 1885, and soon was buffeted by a terrible North Atlantic storm. She did not reach New York Harbor until June 17.

8
AMERICAN TROUBLES

t the climax of years of effort and struggle, the Statue of Liberty almost failed to find a home in America. And the fault was entirely that of the Americans.

American patrons of the project included many prominent persons—Evarts, La Farge, John Jay, Richard Butler. But they did not include a single person of great wealth such as a Gould or Vanderbilt. Many of the patrons could devote little time to fund raising. Evarts, for example, was engaged in trying to end the reign of the corrupt Tweed Ring in New York politics. And all their efforts seemed inept.

When the French took the responsibility for creating the statue, it had seemed a fair division to leave the pedestal and foundation to the Americans. But then Americans began to ask why the pedestal of a figure should cost as much as the figure itself.

There was little public understanding of how important was the pedestal of a monument the size of the Statue of Liberty. A pedestal can do significant things to a work of sculpture: dwarf it or make it seem too large or precariously balanced. Americans were interested in monuments of modest size and simple meaning; the Statue of Liberty seemed too big and complex for them to comprehend. To people of that time the pedestal of a statue seemed like the frame of a painting. It was incomprehensible to them that a frame should cost as much as a painting itself. Even when the cost of the pedestal was whittled to $300,000, few wanted to contribute to it.

The Americans did not show merely apathy. Many were downright antagonistic. This had first been apparent in 1877 when the sponsors had a very hard time persuading Congress even to accept the statue as a gift and provide a site for it. Again, in 1883, when work on the base threatened to collapse from lack of money, Congress refused to pass a bill appropriating $100,000 to it. In 1884 the New York Legislature did approve a grant of $50,000 to the monument, but then Governor Grover Cleveland vetoed it.

Fund-raising efforts around the country outside New York City were mostly laughed at. There seemed to be little sense of national pride when it came to a project that made only one city appear to benefit. It was New York's monument, let New York pay for it. The cost was no more than that of the private car of many a railroad president. Numerous wealthy Americans in New York or elsewhere could have defrayed the cost by signing a check and not felt the difference.

But no rich person would sign a big check. Wealthy people who were importing millions of dollars worth of European art into their private homes and museums would not give $100 to the Statue of Liberty. These self-made millionaires were as suspicious of that word *liberty* as the aristocrats of France had been before the Revolution. Liberty for themselves and their families and

[71]

their friends, yes. But if too much of that liberty was spread among too many people it could start ideas that would be detrimental to the way the millionaires thought the country should be run. Instead of coming right out and expressing their fears, however, the rich mostly just poked fun at Liberty as a bad work of art.

In short, most of the American rich of those days, unlike some rich Americans today, had no sense of social responsibility, no wish to make their money benefit or give pleasure to others. It was all the more surprising that no wealthy donor could be found because the architect chosen to design the pedestal of Liberty was a great favorite with wealthy Americans.

He was Richard M. Hunt, famed for the opulent houses—they were virtually palaces—he designed for American multimillionaires in New York and Newport. By 1880, when he began to make drawings for a Liberty pedestal, he had designed many cultural and commercial works. But a fame he did not altogether like was attached to the fact that many newly rich people felt they didn't have a really great mansion unless "Dick" Hunt designed it.

Hunt loved France and was sympathetic to French republican ideas. A New Englander, he was the first American to graduate from the École des Beaux Arts in Paris. Hunt, who had met Bartholdi on his first visit to America, was delighted to undertake the pedestal of Liberty. His first pedestal design was massive in size and rose 114 feet from its foundations in old Fort Wood. But then people began to complain that it was too high a pedestal and thus belittled the statue it was to support. Also, the costs were running far beyond those the Americans had expected. The foundation, which would support the pedestal, was eating money.

Work on the foundation inside the fort was in the charge of General Charles P. Stone, a Civil War veteran and noted engineer. Starting in 1883, Stone's men began to excavate a big square pit at the center of the fort. They

[72]

soon ran into problems with slabs of rock and rubble from the original fort foundation. But at last they finished a massive foundation, a tapered block of concrete 53 feet deep, 91 feet square at the bottom and 65 feet square at the top.

Unexpected extra cost in building this foundation was another reason why Hunt's pedestal, which rests on it, was shortened in height from 114 feet to 89 feet. This completed pedestal, in Trachtenberg's words, "achieves a controlled, rich and plastic composition that realizes the great scale of the site and the colossus, yet maintains the subordinate silhouette and posture of a pedestal."

Within the pedestal are two sets of massive steel beams to which are locked Eiffel's steel skeleton for the statue. The steel and concrete linking of foundation, pedestal and statue is so strong it has been said that in order to overturn the statue, you would have to overturn the island itself.

But in the early spring of 1885, while Liberty was still in Paris, it seemed that this wonderful structure never would become a reality on Bedloe's Island. Contributions had come to a halt. The Americans were still $100,000 short of their necessary goal, and it appeared that not a penny more could be squeezed from the public.

Remarkable men had been involved in the Statue of Liberty project—Bartholdi, Eiffel, Hunt, General Stone. And now yet another remarkable man appeared to try to save the project from certain death. His name was Joseph Pulitzer, a Hungarian immigrant who had fought in the Civil War and then became a successful journalist. After marrying a wealthy woman, Pulitzer bought the St. Louis *Post-Dispatch*. Then, in 1883, he bought a financial newspaper called the *World* from financier Jay Gould and turned it into a daily for working people.

When Pulitzer heard that the Statue of Liberty was about to die from want of money he resolved to do something about it. His reasons were mixed. He sincerely believed in the Statue as a great memorial to liberty, a symbol of freedom such as he wished for everyone. At the same time Pulitzer saw that he could build the circulation of his newspaper with a campaign to raise money for the monument.

The *World* began running a series of stories about the threat to the Statue of Liberty in March 1885, two months before *Isere* sailed with its dismantled parts. Editorials blasted the rich for their selfish indifference. This increased the paper's circulation among working people, who always enjoyed seeing the rich take a roasting. Then Pulitzer's writers began to needle some of the better-off readers, asking why didn't *they* contribute to Liberty's cause. A fund goal of $100,000 was set. Other New York newspapers, jealous of the *World's* growing circulation, did nothing to help the cause. In fact, the *Times* jeered louder than ever at Liberty. But gradually Pulitzer's writers planted in American minds the idea that this was not a monument just for New York City, but one that belonged to the whole nation. The fund began to grow. But it would not have grown as large and fast as it did if the *World* had not cleverly published the name of every contributor—even the child who could afford only a penny or two. Donors to the campaign totaled more than 121,000 before it was over.

Readers were moved to contribute as much as they could by such messages as these which they read in the *World:*

A lonely and very aged woman with limited means wishes to add her mite.

We send you $1.00, the money we have saved to go to the circus with.

Inclosed please find five cents as a poor office boy's mite to the pedestal fund.

[74]

From sentences like these in the *World* grew the idea, still widely held, that American schoolchildren paid for most of the Statue of Liberty. Certainly they helped pay for the foundation and pedestal, as French schoolchildren helped pay for the statue. But the entire amount of money was raised by a great variety of people from all walks of life in both nations.

That really was better than if a couple of rich people had written checks to pay for all of it. This way, the Statue of Liberty belonged to just about everybody because nearly everyone had helped pay for it.

9
LIBERTY ARRIVES

Only two months before *Isere* sailed into New York Harbor with her precious cargo on June 17, 1885, all work on Liberty's base and pedestal on Bedloe's Island had been halted for lack of money.

But now Pulitzer and his writers on the *World* had raised enough funds to enable work to resume. The *World* also publicized the arrival of *Isere* so thoroughly that the little vessel had a grand welcome when she entered the harbor. Ninety ships bedecked with flags accompanied her up the bay from Sandy Hook to Bedloe's Island. Whistles blared, guns crashed, bands played, choral groups sang patriotic airs both American and French. Suddenly New York had lost its apathy and turned into a noisy cheering section for the Statue of Liberty.

The Statue of Liberty came to symbolize hope and freedom to millions of immigrants to America from Europe. This photo by S. C. Burden shows how the statue looked to those arriving on Ellis Island as they gazed through guard wiring at nearby Bedloe's Island.

(Museum of the City of New York)

Castle Garden at the tip of Manhattan was the debarkation point for
immigrants before Ellis Island was opened. This wood engraving from
The Illustrated London News of September 17, 1864, depicts recruiters
trying to enlist immigrants in the Union Army during the Civil War.
(Museum of the City of New York)

Crossing the Atlantic on a crowded immigrant ship was an excursion in misery. One of the first glimpses of the New World for these people arriving in 1890 was the Statue of Liberty.

(*Museum of the City of New York*)

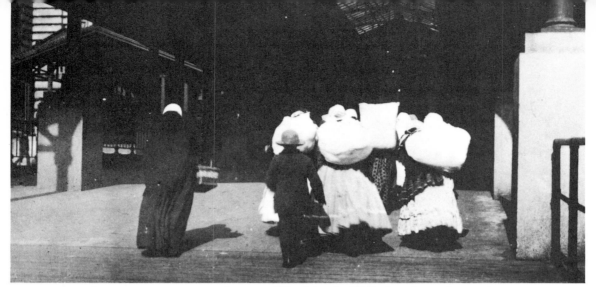

Immigrants coming ashore at Ellis Island. Will they be welcomed to the Promised Land? *(National Archives)*

In this 1907 photo by Burt G. Phillips, these immigrants have been passed by Ellis Island officials and are on their way to New York City. *(Museum of the City of New York)*

This *is* the Promised Land! In this 1901 photograph newly arrived immigrants load themselves, their hopes and all their earthly possessions onto a cart which will take them to tenements in the slums.
(Photographed by Byron from the Byron Collection, Museum of the City of New York)

Then, on August 11, 1885, the *World* proclaimed in a banner headline: ONE HUNDRED THOUSAND DOLLARS!

Every reader knew what it meant. Many felt personal joy, as if they had paid off their family's mortgage.

After the huge, strong base was completed, work on the pedestal proceeded slowly and methodically. The pedestal was not finally finished until April 1886. In the mortar of its last stone a number of pennies, nickels and dimes were scattered, symbolizing the kind of gifts that had made it possible to finish the monument.

Next, the task of raising Eiffel's great steel skeleton was begun. It should have been a simple job, but some of the pieces had been mislaid during the year since they arrived aboard *Isere*. It took two months before the completed gaunt skeleton thrust against the sky like the rigging of a very tall ship.

On July 12 a ceremony on Bedloe's Island marked the riveting of the first piece of copper on the statue. The first rivet was named Bartholdi, the second, Pulitzer. The names of Eiffel, Hunt, General Stone and others who had contributed to the effort followed.

All told, more than 600,000 rivets had to be carefully driven to attach some 300 great pieces of copper to the iron straps fastening the skin of Liberty to its steel skeleton. Seventy-five craftsmen swarmed high above the harbor, swinging perilously on aerial platforms and seats to perform the intricate work. Asbestos insulation had to be fitted at every spot where copper and iron were joined. Otherwise the copper would corrode and crumble in the moist sea air. Eiffel also warned that without such insulation Liberty might turn into a huge electric battery that would shock her visitors. There was no danger of her being damaged by lightning, because copper lightning rods soldered to the inside of the statue would conduct any charges into the ground below.

At last the date of October 28, 1886, was set for the dedication ceremonies. Congress finally opened the public purse enough to allow a sum of $56,500 for the ceremony (with the proviso none of it be spent on alcoholic beverages) and for maintenance of the monument as a lighthouse. In order to light Liberty's beacon, the American Electric Manufacturing Company generously gave an electric plant. Grover Cleveland, who had forbidden $50,000 in state aid to the statue two years previously when governor of New York, now as president of the United States proudly invited French and American officials to attend "Inaugural Ceremonies of Liberty Enlightening the World."

At first it seemed that Bartholdi might not be able to attend the ceremony. His Mama was ill and he did not want to leave her, but Madame said she would be all right and he *had* to go. So he and Jeanne-Emilie boarded a ship and arrived in New York a few days before the big celebration.

When they came into the harbor they could not see anything because of a dense fog. De Lesseps, builder of the Suez Canal who was now interested in building a similar canal across the Isthmus of Panama in order to link the Atlantic and Pacific oceans, traveled to New York with them. His thirteen-year-old daughter Tototte accompanied him. Eiffel had been too busy with other projects to make the trip, so de Lesseps was to fill in for him. The Bartholdis and the de Lesseps family were hustled aboard a yacht the day after their arrival to go out to Bedloe's Island for a look at Liberty.

But the harbor still was soaked in fog. They could not see even the pedestal of the statue as they cruised close to Bedloe's. Bartholdi fumed until his friend Richard Butler, one of the party aboard the yacht, told him to stop fussing. "Auguste," he said, "your statue is there just the way you created it." He took Bartholdi below for some coffee while Jeanne-Emilie and Tototte de Lesseps remained on deck. Suddenly the fog lifted, revealing Liberty in all her copper glory with face masked by a great tricolored sheet, which would not be removed until the dedication ceremony.

[83]

Jeanne-Emilie let out a scream and pointed. On Liberty's raised right arm—modeled after Jeanne-Emilie's own lovely arms—was a wart, a boil, something that should not have been there. Tototte de Lesseps, whose eyes were sharper, laughed and pointed out that it was no blemish. It was a craftsman suspended on a swing ladder who was making a final check of the arm's rivetings. The two called down to Auguste to hurry up and see his Miss Liberty. But by the time he came on deck, fog had obscured the statue again. Bartholdi was destined not to see his work of art at close hand until the day of its unveiling.

The great day, Thursday, October 28, 1886, was officially proclaimed "Bartholdi Day." It dawned raw and rainy, typical fall weather in New York. But rain did not dampen the ardor of the throngs turning out for the festivities. New Yorkers seemed to have gone crazy over the Statue of Liberty.

One million elbowed each other along five miles of streets to watch the biggest parade in the city's history. President Cleveland and members of his Cabinet arrived by special train from Washington. The French ambassador and numerous French dignitaries were there. The governor of New York and his staff were there. Everybody was there—even the very rich, including an Astor and J. P. Morgan, who had done nothing about Liberty when she needed their aid most. Now they vied with one another for seats of prominence in the Madison Square reviewing stand.

New York, reported the *World*, "was one vast cheer." Along the parade route it also was a vast sea of soggy bunting and French tricolors and American stars and stripes. In the parade itself marched 20,000 members of the armed forces, veterans of the Grand Army of the Republic, bands of every description, school groups, patriotic societies. Nearly everybody who wasn't watching was marching through the rain. Indeed, the parade took so long to pass the reviewing stand that the city's official luncheon had to be canceled so that the dignitaries could scurry over to the East River and board vessels to watch a naval parade down the harbor.

Bands blared, whistles blasted, guns boomed and the rain kept falling to the apparent discomfort of no one. While the naval ships were going down the harbor, the marchers and floats still were making their way along Broadway. People began leaving the line of march to go down to the Battery at the southern tip of Manhattan. There the people were so densely packed that a less solid island than old Manhattan might have sunk under their combined weight.

Through the rain the people at the Battery could dimly make out the Statue of Liberty. Hawkers with binoculars did a thriving business: "Here you go! Take a look at Miss Liberty! Five cents for five minutes!" Those who looked saw that she was indeed there, but they couldn't see much else.

The people at the Battery were mainly the ordinary folk who had paid for the Statue of Liberty. The people aboard the official boats going out to Bedloe's Island included some who had done everything for the statue and her pedestal and foundation; they also included many rich men who had done practically nothing about the monument but now had used influence to be in the official party.

Nothing can describe the nature of the times more eloquently than the fact that women were excluded from attending the unveiling ceremony on the island. The only two women allowed to be present were Jeanne-Emilie Bartholdi and Tototte de Lesseps. The official reason given for excluding women was that they might get hurt in the crowd on the small island. But it was common practice to keep women out of many ceremonies in those days. It was a man's world.

Then, as now, however, men found it impossible to repress all women at all times. Women had already started what was called the Suffrage Movement to win the right to vote—which would not come about until well into the next century in the United States. That Suffrage Movement of the nineteenth century was a forerunner of women's present-day efforts toward equal rights for both sexes. On the day the Statue of Liberty was unveiled, many women were understandably annoyed at not being allowed to attend the ceremony. Members of the New York State Woman Suffrage Association refused to be put down. They chartered a boat, loaded it with women and ordered the captain to sail as close to Bedloe's Island as he dared. It was before the days of electronic loudspeakers, so a person with the strongest voice was the most widely heard. That rainy afternoon as the men on the island listened to preachers praying and politicians braying, they could not help but hear a woman speaker aboard the boat who seemed to have a more powerful voice than any man around. She was loudly praising the embodiment of liberty as a woman and saying what a shame it was that if Liberty came to sudden life she would not be allowed to vote in either France or the United States.

Bartholdi was not with Jeanne-Emilie and Tototte among the ranks of solemn men at the foot of Liberty. He was perched high up in the beacon where visitors are not allowed to go today. His role in the ceremony was to pull a cord that would release the huge tricolor covering the face of his statue. He was to pull the cord at a signal from a boy on the ground 300 feet below. This signal would come when Evarts finished his presentation speech to President Cleveland.

Evarts was one of the great and long-winded orators of his time. But even he had to pause for breath once in a while. He had got out only a couple of sentences when he paused to take a deep breath. The eager boy thought he had finished his speech and gave Bartholdi the signal.

Bartholdi tugged the cord and the great tricolor fell aside, revealing the gleaming copper face of Liberty. The ships around the island began to blast

[86]

whistles, guns roared in salute, bands began to play. Evarts clasped his hands to his head in despair and sat down.

President Cleveland was not the great orator that Evarts was said to be. But he spoke some of the most eloquent words of his life after the noise died down and he rose to accept the monument:

"We will not forget that Liberty has made here her home, nor shall her chosen altar be neglected. Willing votaries will constantly keep alive its fires and these shall gleam upon the shores of our sister Republic in the East. Reflected thence and joined with answering rays, a stream of light shall pierce the darkness of ignorance and man's oppression until Liberty enlightens the world."

10
CHANGING
TIMES

The only survivor from the great day of unveiling is Liberty herself. In 1904 Bartholdi died of tuberculosis after designing his own tombstone with the same zest he brought to every task. His mother had died a dozen years before, waited on to the end by the patient daughter-in-law she once had disliked. Jeanne-Emilie lived on many years after Bartholdi's death, long enough to see his beloved Colmar returned to France after Germany's defeat in World War I.

The Statue had a close call in 1916 when a tremendous ammunition explosion on Black Tom Wharf only a half mile away leveled buildings all around New York Harbor. Though Liberty's heart might have skipped a beat, she suffered no serious damage and her beacon did not even blink. Bartholdi, after all, had said she would last forever.

The Statue of Liberty has presided over many joyous occasions. Here she is during Operation Sail on July 4, 1976. The view is down the harbor with the Verrazano Bridge in the background.

(United Press International Photo)

Yet, as with anyone or anything that long endures, the passage of time brought tribulations to Liberty. Life has changed unbelievably since 1886. The Statue was invaded and "seized" on a couple of occasions by groups seeking to publicize their political goals. All types of commercial enterprises have employed the Statue as a symbol to advertise their wares, perhaps the most tasteless being a company that uses a picture of it to promote an underarm deodorant. And highbrow critics have never ceased to lambaste Liberty as a work of art. They complain that it's an artistic hodgepodge, that Bartholdi lacked originality and borrowed from artists of the past; some have even maintained that the Statue offers no personal message to its viewers.

Innumerable people, however, have found a deeply personal message in the Statue of Liberty. For decades it symbolized the hope, haven and humanity of millions of arriving immigrants. In 1892, when the federal government took over from the states the responsibility for immigration, the reception center was moved from Manhattan's Castle Garden to buildings constructed on Ellis Island, almost in the shadow of the Statue. These millions trod American soil for the first time there, inspiring the poet Emma Lazarus to write words memorialized today in a fascinating museum located under the feet of the Statue:

. . . Give me your tired, your poor,
Your huddled masses yearning to breathe free,
The wretched refuse of your teeming shore.
Send these, the homeless, tempest-tost to me,
I lift my lamp beside the golden door!

In 1956 a wish of Bartholdi's finally was realized when the name of Bedloe's Island was officially changed to Liberty Island. Liberty Island and Ellis Island, whose reception services were closed in 1954 after immigration was sharply curtailed, became national monuments in the care of the National Park Service.

Over the years the chief enemy of the Statue of Liberty has been the weather. Buffeted by nearly a century of storms and air pollution, the harbor lady's copper golden mantle became a sickly green. Exposure to the gritty air and corrosive salt also damaged the internal structure of the Statue. Starting in 1983, a team of engineers, architects and government specialists analyzed what repairs were necessary to restore the national monument to its former splendor and safety. They found that the torch needed to be removed and rebuilt to correct leaks. A weak connection of the right arm to the internal pylon had to be reworked. The corroded iron framework of the crown and unsafe handrails on the stairs needed replacement. The discolored copper exterior needed restoration. In order to combat interior humidity, air conditioning and ventilation should be installed. Finally, all of the interior paint had to be stripped, corrosion removed, and the entire structure repainted.

Recognizing the symbolic significance of this great national monument, President Ronald Reagan appointed a special commission in 1984 to "save, restore and preserve" the Statue of Liberty. Head of the Statue of Liberty-Ellis Island Centennial Commission was Lee A. Iacocca, Chairman of the Chrysler Corporation, who had personal feelings about the project as deep as those of so many other Americans.

"My father," Iacocca recalled, "was among the seventeen million immigrants who first saw this great symbol when he arrived in America, penniless, over eighty years ago. He was twelve years old. He went to work. He educated himself. He served his country in World War I. And he built a new life here. The second time he passed the Statue was as an American citizen, bringing with him his new bride, my mother. Though wracked with typhoid fever, she came up on deck to see the torch of welcome as they entered New York Harbor."

With customary driving energy, Iacocca set about raising $45 million to refurbish the Statue, Liberty Island and some of the deteriorated immigration installations on Ellis Island. The major work on the Statue itself would be completed in time for an elaborate centennial celebration on July 4, 1986.

Americans gave more generously than they had a century previously. The leading fund raiser was the Statue of Liberty Ellis Island Foundation, Inc., with headquarters in New York. There were also funding efforts by other organizations such as the French-American Committee for Restoration of the Statue of Liberty, based in Washington, D.C. As scaffolding was raised around the Statue and refurbishing proceeded, visitors continued to use the regular ferry service to travel to the island in large numbers. Although they could not climb into the Statue while repairs were in progress, they were as eager as ever to see as much as possible.

Iacocca offered an explanation for this enthusiasm when describing his own family's experience, typical of that of many others: "The goals of my parents, like those of every other immigrant, were really very simple. They only wanted to provide an opportunity for their families and children to improve themselves. And in doing so, they established a spirit of freedom that prevails in no other country in the world. To me, this project gives us a chance to honor those who came before us and the values they cherished: individual enterprise, hard work and voluntary sacrifice. And, more important, it makes it possible to save the Statue."

Saved it was, to become the focus of happy celebration in the centennial year of 1986. As a national monument the Statue of Liberty remains glorious in the way that Bartholdi intended. She has been called one of the great wonders of the world. The meaning of her existence has varied among various people at different times. But those who visit her today seem to take their greatest delight in the fact that she exists at all.

Acknowledgments

The Statue of Liberty by Marvin Trachtenberg (New York: The Viking Press, 1976) offers a thorough, scholarly study of the conception and building of the statue by a noted architectural scholar. *Statue of Liberty* by Oscar Handlin and the editors of the Newsweek Book Division (New York: Newsweek, 1971) is a handsomely illustrated book which stresses the statue as a symbol of immigration into the United States. *Bartholdi and the Statue of Liberty* by Willadene Price (copyright 1959, but with no recorded publisher) gives an informative, entertaining account of Bartholdi's life. *The Tallest Tower: Gustave Eiffel and the Belle Epoque* by Joseph Harriss (Boston: Houghton, Mifflin, 1975) is a lively biography of the man who developed the skeleton of the Statue of Liberty.

For the background of the Franco-Prussian War, I depended mainly on a previous book of my own, *Legion of Strangers: The Vivid History of a Unique Military Tradition—The French Foreign Legion* (New York: Holt, Rinehart & Winston, 1964). My chief sources for French political and social history were *France* by Albert Guérard (Ann Arbor: University of Michigan Press, 1959) and *The French Nation from Napoleon to Pétain* by D. W. Brogan (New York: Harper, 1957). The chief sources for American social history were *The Americans: A Social History of the United States 1587-1914* by J. C. Furnas (New York: G. P. Putnam's Sons, 1969) and *Everyday Life in the Age of Enterprise 1865-1900* by Robert H. Walker (New York: G. P. Putnam's Sons, 1967).

CHARLES MERCER

INDEX